Contents

KU-130-406

Some words are shown in bold, **like this**. You can find out what they mean by looking in the glossary.

Why experiment?

Where do clouds come from? Why do dogs pant? How does rock turn into lava? What makes chocolate so delicious to eat? You can answer all these questions by investigating what happens when you **heat** or **cool** materials!

Scientists ask questions like these. They work out the answers with the help of **experiments**. An experiment is a test that has been carefully planned to help answer a question.

Get your ears, eyes, nose and hands ready! You'll need to observe your experiments carefully and record what you see, hear, smell or feel.

E s

HE ND
COOLING

Isabel Thomas

raintree

Raintree is an imprint of Capstone Global Library Limited, a company incorporated in England and Wales having its registered office at 7 Pilgrim Street, London, EC4V 6LB – Registered company number: 6695582

www.raintree.co.uk
myorders@raintree.co.uk

Edited by Clare Lewis and Amanda Robbins
Designed by Steve Mead
Picture research by Eric Gohl
Production by Victoria Fitzgerald
Originated by Capstone Global Library Ltd
Printed and bound by CTPS in China

ISBN 978 1 406 29033 2 (hardback)
18 17 16 15 14
10 9 8 7 6 5 4 3 2 1

ISBN 978 1 406 29045 5 (paperback)
19 18 17 16 15
10 9 8 7 6 5 4 3 2 1

British Library Cataloguing in Publication Data
A full catalogue record for this book is available from the British Library.

Acknowledgements
We would like to thank the following for permission to reproduce photographs: Shutterstock: Alena Ozerova, 23 (top right), Asmus, 10 (top), Jaroslaw Grudzinski, 22, MJTH, 23 (top left), Pablo Hidalgo, 10 (bottom), Rob Marmion, 4, V. J. Matthew, 17 (top), Vadym Zaitsev, 21

All other photographs were created at Capstone Studio by Karon Dubke.

We would like to thank Patrick O'Mahony for his invaluable help in the preparation of this book.

Every effort has been made to contact copyright holders of material reproduced in this book. Any omissions will be rectified in subsequent printings if notice is given to the publisher.

All the Internet addresses (URLs) given in this book were valid at the time of going to press. However, due to the dynamic nature of the Internet, some addresses may have changed, or sites may have changed or ceased to exist since publication. While the author and publisher regret any inconvenience this may cause readers, no responsibility for any such changes can be accepted by either the author or the publisher.

Safety instructions for adult helper
The experiments in this book should be planned and carried out with adult supervision. Certain steps should only be carried out by an adult – these are indicated in the text. Always follow the instructions carefully, and take extra care when using a hob (p6), hot tap water (p24) or a knife (p12). Always supervise children when using water from the hot tap for experiments. Do not use boiling water for experiments. Remember that ice cubes can be a slipping hazard if they fall on the floor, and that burst balloons can be a choking hazard. The publisher and author disclaim, to the maximum extent possible, all liability for any accidents, injuries or losses that may occur as a result of the information or instructions in this book.

The experiments in this book will help you to understand how heating and cooling affects materials. You'll learn how to work like a scientist, and have lots of fun along the way!

IS IT A FAIR TEST?

Most experiments involve changing something to see what happens. Make sure you only change one thing, or variable, at a time. Then you will know that it was the variable you changed that made the difference. This is called a fair test.

WARNING! Very hot or cold things can be dangerous. Ask an adult to help you plan and carry out each experiment. Follow the instructions carefully. Look out for this sign.

ADULT HELP

Follow these steps to work like a scientist.

Ask a question.

Come up with an idea to test.

Plan an experiment.

What will you change?
What will you keep the same?
What will you measure?

Make a **prediction**.

Observe carefully.

Work out what the results mean.

Answer the question!

What is it?

Everything in the world is a **solid**, a **liquid** or a **gas**. These are called the three **states of matter**.

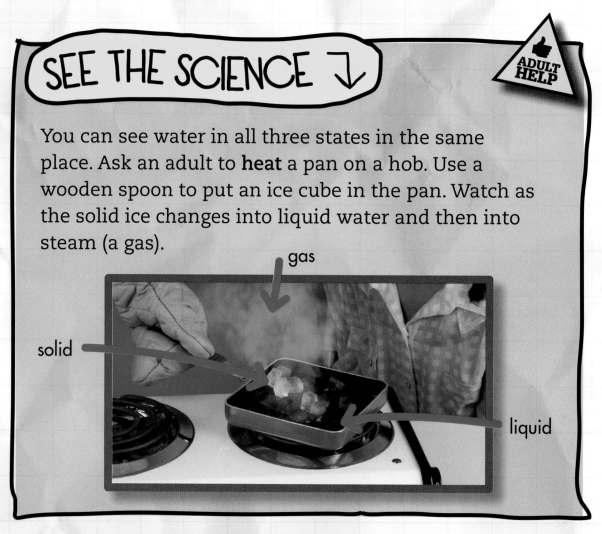

SEE THE SCIENCE ⬇

ADULT HELP

You can see water in all three states in the same place. Ask an adult to **heat** a pan on a hob. Use a wooden spoon to put an ice cube in the pan. Watch as the solid ice changes into liquid water and then into steam (a gas).

gas

solid

liquid

Solids, liquids and gases behave differently (they have different **properties**). Some of the properties are listed in the table on the next page. Use it to help you decide whether the things around you are solids, liquids or gases (or a mixture of these).

Solid, liquid or gas?

Solid	Liquid	Gas
Stays in one place: easy to hold and control	Runny: hard to hold and control because it flows downwards	Flows easily: escapes if it's not trapped in a container: hard to control
Keeps its shape	Changes its shape: spreads out to fill the bottom of its container	Completely fills its container and take its shape
Always takes up the same amount of space (**volume** stays the same)	Always takes up the same amount of space (volume stays the same)	Spreads out to fill a container (volume can change)
Can be cut or shaped	Can be poured easily	Can be squashed so it takes up less space

REAL WORLD SCIENCE

Liquids can be poured. Small pieces of a solid can be poured too, but they form a pile instead of a puddle.

Belt-busting balloons

What happens when you **heat** or **cool** a gas? Let's trap some air (a gas) inside balloons and find out.

EQUIPMENT

- Three balloons
- Balloon pump (or strong pair of lungs)
- Freezer
- Toilet roll
- Marker pen
- Sticky tape
- Glass jug or bowl
- Hot water from a hot tap

Method

1   Blow up and tie the balloons.

2   Wrap a thin "belt" of toilet roll around the fattest part of each balloon. Stick the ends together, making each belt as tight as possible. Number the balloons

3   Put balloon 1 in a freezer. Leave balloon 2 in the room where you blew them up.

4 Ask an adult to fill the jug two-thirds full with hot water from the hot tap. Carefully place balloon 3 on top of the jug and hold it in place. What happens?

5 Look at the balloons after 10 minutes. What has happened to each balloon? What has happened to each belt? Record your results.

6 Draw a table to record your results.

	Balloon 1	Balloon 2	Balloon 3
Where	Freezer	Room	Over a jug of hot water
What happened to the balloon?			
What happened to the belt?			

IS IT A FAIR TEST?

You should only change one thing – the temperature of the balloons. Everything else should stay the same. How can you make sure each balloon starts with the same amount of air?

Conclusion

When a balloon was cooled, its belt got looser. When a balloon was heated, its belt got tighter and broke. The balloons were tied tightly, so no air could escape or get in. They changed size because heating air makes it **expand**, and cooling air makes it **contract**. The air that stayed the same temperature did not contract or expand, so the belt stayed the same.

Freezing and melting

In the last **experiment**, you changed the size of a **gas** by **heating** and **cooling** it. **Solids** and **liquids** also **expand** when they are heated and **contract** when they are cooled.

From gas to liquid
What if you could keep cooling air until it was much colder than a freezer? This would happen! It would turn to liquid.

If you cool air enough, it becomes a liquid.

Heating or cooling can cause materials to change **state**.

From solid to liquid
Look back to page 6. Heating a solid (ice) changed it into a liquid (water). This change is called **melting**. Ice starts to melt at 0°C, but different solids melt at different temperatures.

Look back to page 6.

REAL WORLD SCIENCE

Even rock melts if it gets hot enough. This liquid rock is flowing from a volcano.

From liquid to solid

Cooling a liquid can cause it to change into a solid.
This is called **freezing**. The **freezing point** of water
is 0°C, the same as the **melting point** of ice.

SEE THE SCIENCE ⬇

Ask an adult to melt some solid chocolate over a pan
of simmering water. Liquid chocolate has different
properties from solid chocolate. You can pour it, paint
with it, and change its shape.

Let the chocolate cool. It changes back into a solid.
Changes of state are **reversible** – they can be undone.

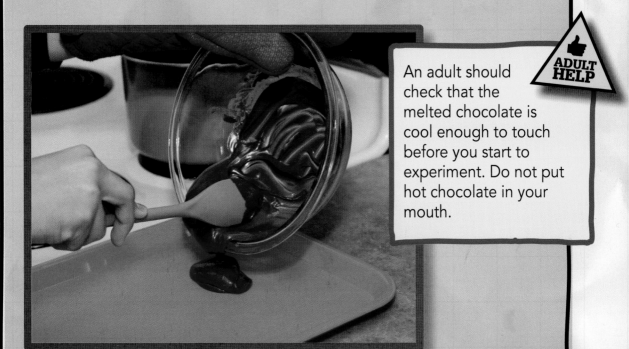

ADULT HELP

An adult should
check that the
melted chocolate is
cool enough to touch
before you start to
experiment. Do not put
hot chocolate in your
mouth.

Pool party

Heating a solid can cause it to melt into a liquid. Do some solids melt faster than others? Host a kitchen pool party to find out.

EQUIPMENT

- Large bowl
- Water from hot and cold taps
- Small foil baking cases
- Different household substances, such as butter, margarine, hard cheese, soft cheese, chocolate, wax and ice
- Butter knife
- Thermometer

Method

1. Cut, break or scoop a small piece of each material into a foil baking case.

IS IT A FAIR TEST?

Make sure each piece is the same size.

If you need to use a knife, ask an adult for help.

ADULT HELP

2. Put a few centimetres of warm water (around 30°C) into the large bowl. Measure and record the temperature of the water.

3. Float the foil cases on the water. Watch carefully. Do any of the materials start to melt? Record what happens.

4. Record your results in a table. This will make it easier to compare them.

Material being tested	Temperature of water		
	30°C	40°C	50°C
Butter			
Hard cheese			
Chocolate			
Soap			

5 Repeat the **experiment** using warmer water (around 40°C). What happens this time? Record what you see.

6 Ask an adult to help you repeat the **experiment** using water straight from the hot tap and water that has been **heated** in a kettle. Record what you see.

Hot water can be dangerous. Always ask an adult for help.

ADULT HELP

7 **Analyse** your results. Which materials started to **melt**? Did this happen at different temperatures?

Body temperature is 37°C. Can you **predict** which of the foods would melt in your mouth?

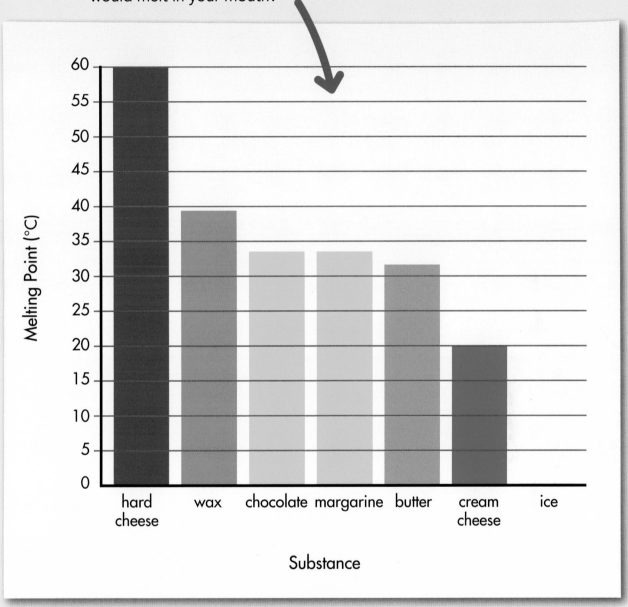

Conclusion

Different materials melt at different temperatures. We say they have different **melting points**. Foods that melt between 30°C and 40°C are **solid** at room temperature, but melt in your mouth. As they melt, they release flavour onto your tongue. This is what makes chocolate so delicious to eat!

Evaporation and condensation

Heating a **solid** can **melt** it into a **liquid**. What happens if you keep heating the liquid?

From liquid to gas

Heating a liquid can cause it to change into a **gas**. This change is called **evaporation**. Water starts boiling if you heat it to 100°C. It quickly changes into steam.

Steam is a mixture of hot gas and tiny droplets of water.

Liquids can also **evaporate** without boiling. Puddles evaporate using heat from the Sun. The water slowly changes into a gas called water vapour. We can't see the water vapour, but it does not disappear. It goes into the air.

Hold a wet finger up in the air. What do you see and feel? Your finger dries as the water evaporates. A liquid can only evaporate if it takes heat from somewhere. The water takes heat from your finger. This makes your finger feel colder.

Water takes heat from the dog's tongue as it evaporates. This helps to cool the dog down.

From gas to liquid

Like other changes of **state**, evaporation is **reversible**. When water vapour cools, it turns back into liquid water. This change is called condensation.

Breathe on to a mirror. What do you see? Water vapour in your breath cools when it touches the mirror. It changes into tiny drops of liquid water.

Weather in a jar

How does **heating** and **cooling** affect the world's water? Make a **water cycle** inside a jar and find out!

EQUIPMENT

- Glass jar
- Water from hot tap and cold tap
- Measuring jug
- Foil tray or dish large enough to cover the jar
- Clingfilm
- Ice cubes
- Torch
- Timer

Method

1 Put a few centimetres of warm water into the glass jar. Cover the top of the jar with clingfilm.

2 Put a handful of ice cubes into the foil tray. Put the tray on top of the jar. Start the timer.

3 What happens inside the jar? Lift the foil tray off the jar every few minutes to look at the clingfilm. Record everything you see. Write down the time that it happens.

4 Repeat steps 1 to 3 using **cooler** water. What happens? Record what you see and how long it takes.

Hot water can be dangerous. Always ask an adult for help.

ADULT HELP

5 Finally, repeat steps 1 to 3 using water from a hot tap. Record what you see and how long it takes.

 ## IS IT A FAIR TEST?

You are testing what happens when you change the temperature of the water. Everything else, such as the amount of water in the jar, should stay the same. Make sure you dry the bottom of the foil tray between each **experiment**.

6 Darken the room and shine a torch into the jar. Can you see mist at the top of the jar? Why do you think it forms near the top?

You have made a mini water cycle inside the jar. The water at the bottom of the jar **evaporates**. The water vapour is carried in the air. When it gets near the cold foil, it cools and **condenses**. A "cloud" of tiny water droplets forms. As the droplets get bigger, they 'rain' back into the bottom of the jar.

7 Draw a table of your results, like the example below, to help you **analyse** them.

Temperature of water in jar	Mist	Small drops	Large drops	Drops started to "rain" back into jar
Cold	2 minutes, 30 seconds	10 minutes	30 minutes	1 hour 10 mins
Warm	1 minute	3 minutes	11 minutes	35 minutes
Hot	instant	1 minute	7 minutes	11 minutes

Conclusion

The water in the jar evaporated whether it was cool, warm or hot. We know this because condensation appeared on the clingfilm covering each jar. The warmer the water, the faster it evaporated. This is why puddles and washing dry faster on a warm or sunny day.

You also showed that evaporation is a **reversible** change. The water vapour that formed in the jars turned back into liquid water when it cooled.

Try the experiment using coloured ice cubes. This will help you to prove the drops on the clingfilm come from the water inside the jar.

REAL WORLD SCIENCE

Water cycle

The world's water changes from liquid to gas (and back again) all the time. Water in seas, lakes and rivers evaporates as the Sun heats it. The water vapour rises into the sky, cools, and **condenses** back into liquid. It falls to the ground as rain, snow or hail. This is called the **water cycle**.

Heat on the move

Heat is a form of energy. When you heat a material, you give it more energy.

When heat travels through a material, energy is moved from place to place. Heat always moves from the warmer part of a material to the **cooler** part.

Heat travels easily through some materials. They are called **thermal conductors**. Other materials do not let heat pass through them easily. They are called **thermal insulators**.

REAL WORLD SCIENCE

Metals are good thermal conductors. Pans are made from metal because we want heat to pass through them quickly to cook food. Plastics are good thermal insulators. Pan handles are made from plastic because we want them to stay cool.

Heat energy always moves from hot things to colder things. Which way is heat traveling in these pictures?

SEE THE SCIENCE ↓

Dab a blob of butter at the top of wooden, plastic and metal spoons. Stand the spoons in a jar of hot water. What happens to the butter on each spoon? Heat travels more quickly through good thermal conductors. Which material is the best conductor?

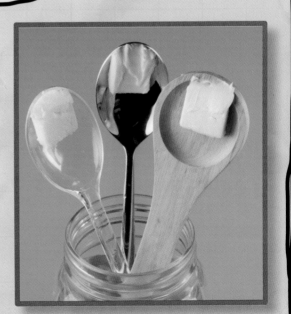

ADULT HELP

Hot water can be dangerous. Ask an adult to heat and pour the water for you.

Ice cream emergency!

Thermal insulators are really useful when we want to trap **heat** in or keep it out. Can you find the best insulator to stop the heat of your hands from **melting** ice cream?

EQUIPMENT

- Four or more empty soft drink cans
- Sheets of three or more different materials, such as bubble wrap, paper, cotton, wool and foam packing material
- Jug of hot tap water
- Plasticine
- Tray
- Thermometer
- Timer

Method

1 Wrap each can in a different material. Leave one unwrapped. Place the cans on a tray.

2   Fill a jug with hot tap water. Measure the temperature of the water. Pour some of the water into each can. Seal each can with plasticine.

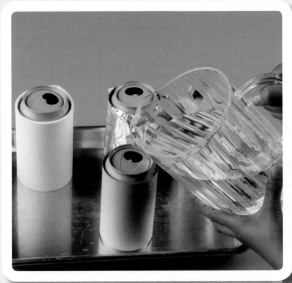

3   Ask an adult to help you put the tray of cans into the fridge. Leave the cans for 10 minutes.

Predict: Which can of water will **cool** down most quickly? Which will keep the water warm for longest?

IS IT A FAIR TEST?

Remember to change just one thing – the material used to wrap the cans. Everything else should stay the same. Make your **experiment** fair by putting the same amount of water in each can and using the same number of sheets of material to wrap each can. Is it a **fair test** if each material is a different colour? How could you improve your experiment?

4 After 10 minutes, measure the temperature of the water in each can. Record the measurements in the table. Seal the cans again.

Ask an adult to help you. Handle the thermometer carefully.

ADULT HELP

5 After another 10 minutes, measure and record the temperature of the water in each can. Keep recording the temperature every 10 minutes until they are all the same temperature.

6 **Analyse** your results. Which can of water **cooled** down most quickly? Which material was best at keeping the **heat** in?

7 Plot the results on a graph. Use a different colour to plot the results for each can. Join your points to make lines.

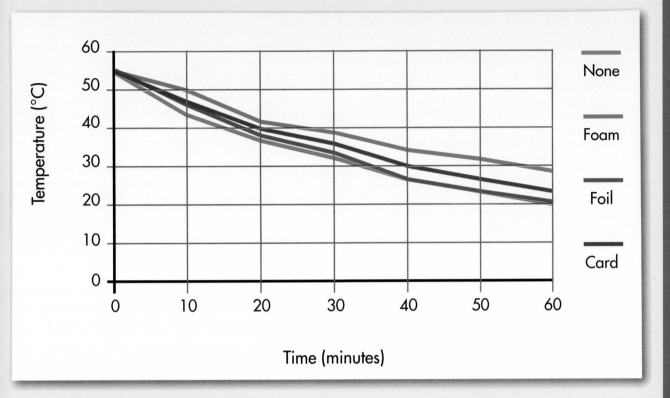

Conclusion

Thermal insulators slow down the flow of heat from a warmer place to a colder one (from the water to the air in the fridge). The best thermal insulator was the one that kept the heat in for the longest time. This would be the best material for an ice cream container, because good insulators keep heat out as well as in.

Wrap your best thermal insulator around a container of ice cream and see how well it keeps out the heat from your hands.

Plan your next experiment

Experiments have helped you discover some amazing things about **heating** and **cooling**. Just like you, scientists carry out experiments to answer questions and test ideas. Each experiment is planned carefully to make it a **fair test**.

YOU ASKED...

YOU FOUND OUT THAT...

How does temperature affect materials?

- **Heating solids, liquids** and **gases** can make them **expand**. Cooling them can make them **contract**.
- Heating and cooling materials can change them from one **state** to another.

How does heating affect solids?

- Heating solids can make them **melt** into liquids.
- Different solids have different **melting points** – they melt at different temperatures.
- Melting is **reversible**. Cooling liquids can make them **freeze** into solids.

How does heating affect liquids?

- Liquids can **evaporate** into gases.
- Heating a liquid makes it evaporate more quickly.
- This change is reversible. Cooling gases can make them **condense** into liquids.

How well does heat travel through different materials?

- Heat energy can move from place to place by travelling through materials.
- Heat travels most quickly through good **thermal conductors**, such as metals.
- **Thermal insulators** do not let heat pass through them easily, keeping heat in *and* keeping it out.

Experiments also lead to new questions! Did you think of more questions about heating and cooling? Can you plan new experiments to help answer them?

What will you discover next?

WHAT NEXT?

→ Does a material weigh the same after it changes state? Can you plan an experiment to find out?

→ Can you plan an experiment to compare the melting points of different types of chocolate?

→ Does the size of a puddle affect evaporation? What about the breeze? Plan an experiment to find out.

→ Do some metals conduct heat better than others? Can you plan an experiment to find out?

Glossary

analyse examine the results of an experiment carefully, in order to explain what happened

condense change from a gas into a liquid

contract get smaller

cool lower the temperature of something

evaporate change from a liquid into a gas

expand get bigger

experiment procedure carried out to test an idea or answer a question

freeze change from a liquid into a solid

freezing point temperature at which a material freezes

gas state of matter when a material changes shape to fill its container, and can expand or be squashed so it takes up a different amount of space

heat raise the temperature of something

liquid state of matter when a material is runny and changes shape to fill the bottom of its container, but always takes up the same amount of space

melt change from a solid into a liquid

melting point temperature at which a material melts

observation noting or measuring what you see, hear, smell or feel

prediction best guess or estimate of what will happen, based on what you already know

property characteristic of a material; how it looks or behaves

reversible can be undone

solid state of matter when a material is firm, does not change shape and always takes up the same amount of space

state (of matter) whether something is a solid, liquid or gas

thermal conductor material that conducts heat well

thermal insulator material that does not conduct heat well

variable something that can be changed

volume amount of space that a material takes up

water cycle how water moves between oceans, Earth's atmosphere and land, changing from liquid to gas and back again

Find out more

Books

Experiments with Solids, Liquids and Gases, Christine Taylor-Butler (Scholastic, 2011)

Science Experiments, Robert Winston (DK, 2011)

Solids, Liquids and Gases (Essential Physical Science), Louise and Richard Spilsbury (Raintree, 2013)

Super Science: Solids, Liquids and Gases, Rob Colson (Franklin Watts, 2013)

Websites

www.bbc.co.uk/schools/scienceclips/ages/8_9/solid_liquids.shtml
Turn solids into liquids – and back again – with this online experiment.

www.miamisci.org/af/sln/phases/coppergas.html
See what happens when you change the temperature of a liquid, solid and gas.

www.sciencebob.com/experiments/
Find more experiments to do at home or school.

Index